No Girlfriends Allowed

Unlearning What You Learned About Love & Relationships

Marcia Alene

Ordering & Booking Information:
Special discounts are available on quantity purchases of books by corporations, associations, and others. For ordering details or to book Marcia Alene for your next speaking engagement, please contact:

marcia@nogirlfriendsallowed.com

1st ed.

ISBN: 978-1-945993-01-5 (print)

DEDICATION

This is far from a "how to get a man" book, nor is this a book of judgment. This is a collection of transparency. The goal of this book is to challenge thoughts and raise questions. This is not just for women but for everyone to appreciate.

I grew up with Christian beliefs, so there will also be references to what I knew in my early life and what I have come to know now. However, this is not just for the religious I want everyone to keep an open mind and enjoy the journey.

Ultimately, we are all doing our best with the knowledge we have at this current moment. So I dedicate this book to people like myself: the lovers of love, hopeless romantics, and all those who do not want to give up on love.

With Pure Love,

ACKNOWLEDGMENTS

Mom, thank you for showing me the meaning of unconditional love. I know what support and selflessness looks like because of you.

Dad, I love you and thank you for being you.

Grandma, thank you for your wise words and always keeping me laughing.

Los, my Dad (I don't like calling you "stepdad"), thank you for your consistent support over the years and for being an example of a provider. I truly appreciate you.

Grandma Annie, thank you for inspiring me to keep pushing to complete this book. Thank you so much for teaching me to chase purpose in everything I do.

I want to thank everybody I have encountered at any moment in my life. Good, bad, and ugly. Every moment was necessary to contribute to the lessons life gave me. I want to thank God, my family, and close friends who have stuck around through times when it was hard to love me. Everything happens for a reason, and today I am here because of you.

TABLE OF CONTENTS

• • • • • • • • ●● ● ●● • • • • • • •

"Every place where you set your foot

will be yours ..."

- Deuteronomy 11:24

• • • • • • • • ●● ● ●● • • • • • •

INTRO

"How can you be a girlfriend when you were raised to be a wife?"

- The question I could never answer

I was sitting in my pastor's office at the age of 14 when I asked him, "What is a girlfriend?" The look on his face told me that he did not have an answer that would make me understand what exactly this label meant. I wanted to know why it existed and where it came from. I told him that I searched from Genesis to Revelation and could not find one "girlfriend." There were plenty of "concubines," but not one "girlfriend." The women were single, married, or as we would say today, "on the side." Yes, throughout the Old Testament, there was the practice of multiple wives, but that was somewhat of a cultural thing based on my understanding of the time. If there was no mention of a girlfriend, then why is that something we practice today? I remember the pastor stating that it was just a step that we took to get to know someone. My next question was, "Why is it a necessary step?" So, needless to say, I was still confused and left it at that.

I never knew what it meant to be a girlfriend, and I definitely didn't know what it should feel like to be one. According to one etymology dictionary, it meant a female friend or a non-committed relationship. What is a non-committed relationship? My mom would always say that I would make a great wife one day, but not a great girlfriend. So that was my focal point: a wife. *Why would anyone aim to be a girlfriend when no one actually knows what it means to be one? If you don't know where it comes from, then how do you know how to act as one? And how long should you be a girlfriend before becoming a wife?* These were all questions swirling around in my head that I couldn't answer. Yep, I am one of those people who asks myself a billion questions!

Finally, at the age of 27, I decided to revisit those swirling questions after having three failed boyfriend/girlfriend relationships, which all felt like marriages but only to a degree we went through the same heartache without the actual committed union. Just like a marriage, I gave my all. 100% of my love, time, devotion, commitment, and trust went into these relationships because I went into them thinking it would last forever. But it never ended up that way. It seems that forever is just another term that is not lived through society's views. As a culture, we can be so selfish sometimes and very quick to give up. And why did I think it was going to be forever? He never proposed. Yes, we talked about the future, but maybe I jumped the gun too soon from day one. There were never any plans made or names changed. The plans were only in my head, nothing was concrete. I'd even imagine how my first name would sound with his last name, but we were doing the most without the most important part: a commitment.

So, what do you do as a *girlfriend* that is different from a *wife*? I asked the pastor for instructions, but it seemed that he did not have the manual handy for me to read over. Now at the age of 27, I decided to do my research for myself after yet another break-up and heartbreak. Everything I always felt about being a girlfriend came rushing back; every thought that I always wondered. *Why am I here again, feeling the same way, and tired of going through the same routine?* The answer was simple: neither I, nor anyone else around me truly understood the process. All we knew is how a wife should be and to date with the goal of marriage. So why was I now so shocked that this cycle would not end, a cycle that seemed like chaos because there was not a happy medium between being single and married? For me, the term "girlfriend" just added an unnecessary complication with the side effects of heartbreak, fatigue, anger, bitterness, and a host of other pains. I wanted to go deeper and really find out what this all really meant and why it was impacting my life the way it was, as well as the lives of others.

Instead of giving up or bringing more pain into the next situation, I decided to take a detox period for myself, which I will go into more detail later. I went through all of my journals since the age of 4 and I saw something consistent in my writing: love. So I started bringing all those journal entries together to figure out what love meant to me today. *No Girlfriends Allowed* began the healing process for me and turned into a rediscovery of life before marriage. After talking to and interviewing so many men and women (single, married, divorced, and widowed) of all ages, I realized the common goal for all: love...unconditional love. It seemed that the vast majority yearned for the same basic needs and foundation. Now the question was, *how do we go through the layers to get there?*

Now before I talk about my goal in the end, let me say that this is for those who do want a monogamous marriage. Yes, I am aware that may not be everyone's goal. I am also not saying this should be put above all things. This is just a goal. You may have a career goal, a financial goal, or a health goal, so there is nothing wrong with having a relationship goal. If you strive to have a monogamous marriage, then so be it. Don't let others put that seed of doubt in you because they do not believe the same.

> **My goal is to simplify where we already are—to simplify the path to marriage, get rid of some confusion, and to get the foundation back into a lot of areas in our lives and lessen the chances of bringing unnecessary pain upon ourselves.**

No one deserves to go through a cycle that feels like there is no end. People should not be on the verge of giving up and losing hope in love. Ultimately, most of us want to give and receive that honest, committed love. The process starts with you and your way of thinking. In order to be happy with another person, you must first be happy with yourself.

No "Pit-Stops" Allowed

"She was not meant to be a girlfriend. She was taught to be a wife. Never attended 'How to be a Girlfriend' seminars. It was more like, 'How to be a Lady' and 'How to be Submissive to Your Husband'. Her mother never told her that she'd make a great **GIRLFRIEND.** *She always said 'You're going to be a great* WIFE'. *So she grew up with the mentality of being a wife, but somewhere along the line, being a girlfriend came along for the ride...and she settled. Settled because she figured 'it MIGHT be right, I mean not really, but why not give it a try?' The world has created this relationship 'pit stop' which says, 'You can be my girlfriend/boyfriend until we decide what we really want to do. I mean, I love you, I do, but I just don't know if I want to marry you.' That's the mentality that the world brought along and that is how many hearts have been torn. When will people get back on board—realizing there is no 'pit-stop'? It's either you're married or you're not!"*

- Karissa Dean

Children's hairstylist and dope individual

CHAPTER 1

I Want the Title

• • • • • • • ● ● ● ● • • • • • •

"I want to be known as your girl…I want to kick it with you like your best friend."

\- "The Title" by Ciara

• • • • • • • • ● ● ● • • • • • •

At 27, I am just realizing what I've been doing consistently throughout my adult life getting wrapped up and letting my life slowly disappear and reappear in the form of a man's life. Unknowingly, I would wrap my time up into theirs. Every break-up resulted in emptiness. Every time, I would have to pick up the pieces of my life I had left behind all over again. I would neglect my goals, my dreams, my friends, and sometimes even my own health. I read a post recently that said, "You know that tingly feeling you get when you start to like someone? That's common sense leaving your body." I chuckled, but for me it was true. All logic would go out the window and emotions would control my thoughts. It was a vicious cycle, a cycle that had to end. Right now, I'm ending that cycle.

I have a freedom that I have never had before. I have never known what it was like to live my own life while also sharing it with the person I was emotionally invested in. I started asking around and spoke to many women who all said the same thing: we stop living our lives, neglect our wants, and try to fill the holes we perceive in our significant others' lives. We cater, we nurture, and we put ourselves last. I understand that is how some women are designed, but I just don't think our nurturing ways were meant for us to go to that extreme. Now not every woman is built that way, and even some men do the same to fill the void in their partners. However, in everything there has to be a balance, a balance I personally was on a journey to find.

But I am still learning. The funny thing is that as I write this, the person I'm involved with currently is not even my boyfriend. How ironic, right? Well that brings me to where I am. I am finally putting myself first. Of course God is my number one, but then there's me! Here's the thing: it is not easy, and it is not natural. My habits have controlled my decisions. I am now taking a conscious effort to change my habits with one of my favorite proverbs, *"for as he thinks in his heart, so is he" (Proverbs 23:7)*. How we think and feel ultimately controls what we see.

One night, a 35-year-old, unmarried woman said, "I don't care if you're married with 10 kids, don't stop having a life!" It was confirmation for me. Giving your all to someone and neglecting yourself can take your life right out from under you without the person you are involved with even being conscious of it. Some people form into selfless or selfish adults. You see, some people are automatically selfish, they are born with a selfish gene a gift in my opinion; they don't have to put extra thought into making the decisions that are best for them. They have to put extra thought into actually considering their mates. I wish it was that easy for me, but it wasn't. I considered the person I was with first in everything without ever thinking about myself. But that too is a gift, being selfless. Yes! It is a gift, not a curse, to embrace and be selfless by nature. But whatever side of the scale you fall on, it's always good to strive for balance. I now know that I have to make a conscious effort to do what is best for me as well. I have to find my selfish gene. That's deeper than a puddle to me, I swear.

Boyfriend/Girlfriend

Now, my next thoughts led me to Google. What's the point of a boyfriend anyway? I have often heard that you are considered single until you're officially married. I know some type of commitment has to be made regardless, but I wonder if this "boyfriend/girlfriend" title ultimately slows us down towards our final destination. Most people I ask, both men and women, want to be married, but the journey we are taking to get there looks like a bunch of blurred lines, in my opinion. I can think of a hundred reasons why, but I will stick to this "title" focus.

In the USA, the term "girlfriend" started in the 1860s. The title referred to a friend or home-girl. I was surprised to learn what I found next: "girlfriend" meant a non-committed relationship. So, all this time, I'm stepping into a non-committed relationship and wondering why things aren't leading me to commitment! Was it ever meant to? Using "girlfriend" in terms of a relationship started in the 1920s, a.k.a. the roaring '20s. Now, a lot was going on during that time, including the introduction of the flapper. A flapper was a young woman, unconventional or without decorum, particularly associated with the 1920s. Before the 1920s, women used to dress very modestly in dresses all the way down to their ankles and had the majority of their bodies covered up. When the 1920s hit, society was booming; people were making a lot of money, operating in the arts, and women received their right to vote, which liberated them, in more ways than one.

> *"The 1920s were marked by the rise of the flapper, a new breed of young Western women who wore short skirts, bobbed their hair, danced to jazz music, and flouted social and sexual norms. Flapper dresses were straight and loose, leaving the arms bare (sometimes no straps at all) and dropping the waistline to the hips. The evolving flapper look required "heavy makeup" in comparison to what had previously been acceptable outside of professional usage in the theater."* (Flapper, 2014)

Now what does that have to do with anything? As we progress as a society, we're looking for balance between patriarchy vs. feminist ideals. It is not uncommon for me to hear someone say, "I just don't believe in marriage anymore." But why is that? Why have so many people given up on marriage and love in its entirety? Ok, maybe the social construct of marriage is a turn-off to some, but at the same time, people still want a partner in crime or love. Nowadays, we do not even have to be girlfriend and boyfriend; we can just "hook up." I'm not saying that this is new, I'm just saying it is more out there with today's media and fast paced society than ever before. We are continuously taking the power away from marriage, and I understand why, especially with how people feel about the government's laws regarding marriage (but I am not going down that rabbit hole). Instead of focusing on a straight path to marriage, we are adding a bunch of "pit-stops." The more stops we add, the further away from marriage we are. I understand marriage is not a goal for everyone, but there are still individuals out there who want and believe in it.

I remember reading one of Myles Munroe's books that described the things that Adam had before Eve stepped onto the scene. You don't have to believe in the Bible, however, it is still a great story. Dr. Munroe spoke on the things Adam had first before meeting his partner. Adam, most of all, had God. He had a home, a purpose, and he cultivated. Not only was he in his purpose, but he was also working in it. He was being productive. I thought to myself, *shouldn't I be doing the same thing?* Now the following is what I believe in the story: I believe that God spent time with Eve as well, before she was presented to Adam. I believe God gave her the scope of what her role was, who she was, and what she needed to do. She didn't just pop up and say, "Hey Adam, I'm ready! Let me focus my whole life on you and your purpose." She was productive and prepared. Dr. Munroe also revealed in a sermon, "Singleness is more important than marriage because your marriage is based on your singleness." This blew my mind. He was showing me that being single (therefore selfish) gives you a foundation of thinking of yourself first so you'll have the habit already in place before you're married, and are therefore more likely to find balance when you join your life with someone else's. That is around the time that my focus shifted towards myself. My level of SELFLESSness deserved more SELFISHness, without the guilt of finally putting myself first. My happiness should be found in me and not sought after in another person.

Marriage is not life, and neither are relationships. Everything is a part of life. Being a lover of love, I tend to care about this topic more than others. This is also the area of my life that I felt I could not get right. I treated all of my relationships like marriages because that is how I believed it should be. I grew up around positive examples of wives. I also understand how never seeing a positive example of marriage can shape your beliefs as well. I never cheated because I find myself to be a loyal person and I do believe that what goes around comes around. I gave my all, but I found that I was not getting the same in return. I always went in with the mentality of "forever," so the thought of ending it was never in my mind; no matter what happened.

As I grew into my adult years, the culture seemed to shift into the "you are either single or married" mind frame. There was no in-between. Well, if you think of it from a government perspective, when you fill out most forms, you check single, married, separated/divorced, or widowed. The "in-between status" seems to come after you are married, not before.

After my last relationship ended (with someone I thought for sure would be my husband), I took some much needed time to myself. I had met a lot of people like myself who had gotten lost in their partners' lives. They were just wives/girlfriends/mothers or husbands/boyfriends/fathers, yet they had no clue who they *really* were. Women and men alike are created for a purpose and an ultimate destiny. I think our first goal in life should be to find out what our own purposes are. Do you know why you are here on this Earth, why you exist? Once we find it, we need to build a foundation on it and execute it. Life, love, and passion comes alive that way with self. Self first.

> **My definition of PURPOSE:**
> **Something you do daily without**
> **thinking about it, or something you**
> **think about daily without doing it.**

This led me to this thought: you can be SINGLE and AVAILABLE or SINGLE and UNAVAILABLE. If you are single and available, you know what you want and you are ready to go after it. You are not dating to pass time with no purpose in it. You know what you want, but you are bettering yourself daily until what you want comes along. You will be able to recognize it because you are already centered. You have already figured out who you are, what your purpose is, and you are in the process of working towards your goals. If you are single and unavailable, you are still working on you. Or, that means you are not creating more broken hearts in others because you do not know what you want yet. You are okay with being by yourself until you figure out what you truly want and need.

You may not know exactly what you want out of life at the moment or what you were called to do on this Earth, but the important thing is that you are aware of where you are and you are moving towards getting to know yourself. You do not have to apologize for being concerned with yourself during this self-evaluation process. Don't put all of your effort into improving someone else when you have not worked on yourself first. It is okay to be selfish while getting into your wholeness, and during this process you have to protect yourself from other's opinions of your personal journey. If you are single and unavailable, for whatever reason, be single and unavailable until you are ready to become single and available.

CHAPTER **2**

Spiritmates

*"I don't believe in soulmates, but I
do believe there is an unexplainable
connection that can exist beyond
physical and emotional."*

- Inner thoughts throughout my life

Here I was at serious relationship number three
in my 20s. It was starting to feel like a routine.
I'd meet someone and take off like a rocket,
only to crash and burn as fast as I started. In the
beginning, everything just felt right, sometimes
surreal a connection that I had a hard time putting
my finger on. I'd feel like I'd met my best friend and

this may be "the one" that I kept hearing about. I'd meet someone who just understood me without me having to explain myself. Sound familiar?

Relationship number three, like every other, was the same. It felt like the same script, *"You're the most amazing woman I have ever met. I prayed for someone like you. I think you're perfect for me."* Insert the phrase that makes you feel like this may be real. When the relationship ended, I was left thinking, *"Well if I am so amazing, why are we here now? If it was 'meant to be,' why does this all feel like a mistake in hindsight? What happened to this prayer you supposedly made? Did that prayer change? So you thought I was perfect for you in the beginning? Do you even remember why we started?"*

Relationship after relationship, I started to doubt my greatness as well as myself. As I got older, my once carefree and confident perception of myself turned into an unhealthy level of nitpicking. I would focus more on my flaws than my great qualities. I started to doubt every little thing as time moved on in a relationship. Instead of thinking about what I could offer in a relationship, I was steadily thinking about everything I did wrong in the past. For example, if he canceled a plan with me or got mad at me for something I thought was minimal, I would blame myself and quickly start apologizing to prevent conflict. Even if I felt like I did nothing wrong, I would put a very unbalanced level of guilt on my shoulders. It even got to the point where I would solely blame myself for something that was caused by the both of us.

I was still confused and I still had questions. How do you come into someone's life intending to waste his or her time? If you see it is not what you want from day one, why not end it?

> **If you are not 100% sure that the person you are dating now will not be your last, stop spitting in the moment falsities that get that person's hopes up.**

If you do not believe in monogamous relationships, find another person who doesn't as well. If you want to be with a person, but that person does not want to be with you, then let it go instead of sticking around off of hope alone.

In the book *The Four Agreements,* one of the

agreements you should make with yourself is to "Be impeccable with your word. Speak with integrity. Say only what you mean. Use the power of your word in the direction of truth and love." What I took from that in regards to dating is to be upfront and stand true to your word. If you want something with someone, be honest about where you stand today. If you are not ready, say it and explain why. Do not say you are not ready as a cop out to do other things and string a person along.

So from that point on, I took responsibility for myself. I cannot control the next person and his actions, I can only acknowledge my part in the situation. I started to recognize when I did not want something and I removed myself without guilt. I also recognized when I stayed too long and when I should have let go. Lastly, I recognized what I truly wanted and could spot it earlier in the "getting to know someone" process.

Soulmates?

So what exactly is "the one" that everyone speaks of? How do you just know that that's the person you're meant to be with forever? The word "soulmate" always interested me. I did not understand why, if the origin of it was from Greek mythology, it was so widely used in the church. The concept of "soulmates" comes from the Greek story in which Zeus cuts people in half, making them have to search for their other halves for the rest of their lives. Cute story I guess; I just didn't believe it. I will say I have come to believe in something I call "spiritmates." First, let me explain what I believe a spirit is. It's simply who we are. We are a spirit first and foremost. I was reading *How to be Led by the Spirit of God* and it broke it down in a way that made sense for me. We are a spirit first, a powerful spirit at that. We are a spirit that is made in the likeness and image of God, not the human God we try to create on this Earth. Our spirit in human form is encompassed by a soul. Our soul is our mind, our will, and our emotions. Our spirit and soul lives in a fleshly body. So we are a spirit, that has a soul, that lives in a body.

Knowing that you are a spirit with a soul that lives in a body, it is very possible to have a spiritmate. Spiritually, you can connect with someone. Yes, you can also be connected to someone's soul. The soul that encompasses your mind, willpower, and emotions, changes too frequently to be connected to someone on the soul level alone. Your feeling today is not going to be your same feeling tomorrow; it's not going to be the same the next year or the year after. A relationship will not last on mere feelings. Feelings are temporary and a foundation on feelings is fickle. And the body, oh, we already know it's possible to hit and quit it! Or simply be drawn to someone physically when nothing else connects. As a spirit, it makes more sense in the biblical concept of becoming ONE with the person you marry on a spiritual foundation, connected by emotions, consummated by flesh.

That made me realize that I had based my thoughts and feelings on "the one" as just that, thoughts and feelings, a.k.a. my soul. The freaking fickle, ever-changing, non-consistent soul determined why the beginning always felt so right but faded over time. I gave myself physically in hopes that it would be enough to keep the person there, not for my pleasure, but to only please him. So I decided to go on a fast with the purpose to get rid of any and all distractions and figure out how to dissect myself as a three-part being. Our spirit being the greatest and most powerful of the three.

Now, I was raised in the church, but I never wanted my ideas to be put in a box. I started off with what I already knew, the Daniel fast. It is a biblical-based and spiritually motivated diet/fast that you do for 10 to 21 days. I did the 3-week period. The option I chose was closer to what Daniel did, which was to eat only plain and simple foods, no seasoning, meat, or wine. I ate just things that grew naturally from the earth, something close to your modern-day vegan. I drank water only.

I learned during the fast that we truly put our bodies first. If we are hungry, we eat, if we are horny, we have sex we are responsive to the flesh. The body is the least of the parts that make up our being, but we respond to it first. We are spiritual, powerful beings first with minds, wills, and emotions, which just so happen to live in a very carnal body. We cater to it first, and we limit the nature of our spirit by putting our carnal needs ahead of the spirit.

Let's put it this way. We are in a constant battle between being our best and truest selves in the now, versus settling with what feels good in the current moment. The spirit is our best, truest selves, and the body is the "in-the-moment," not so best urges we satisfy. Next we have the soul, which I would call the middleman. Which way the middleman sways results in the outcome. Our soul is constantly trying to decide which side to pick. If the middle man sides with the spirit, magic happens, but if it sides with the body, it still may feel like magic but just a little more temporary.

Let me backtrack a little. Around 2012, I was reading the bible and trying to understand the Hebrew and Greek translations to get the full context of the scriptures. At the same time, I was reading *How to be Led by the Spirit of God* and *The Secret* simultaneously. I found myself delving into the self-help book world and seeing that it actually brought the biblical context to life. I felt like a heathen! Okay not really, but I just felt like those around me in the Christian faith would not understand me, and those who knew my walk in what is commonly called the "secular" world would just straight up call me a hypocrite.

Then two years later I watched the movie *Lucy* and I felt like I was the only person in the movie theater who was excited about what I saw! It brought me back to that three-part being. In the movie, Lucy got to the point where she could not feel the physical anymore and transcended everything through spirit. She was connected to everything on this Earth and every piece of energy and vibration. The physical things that would stop her disappeared throughout the movie; she could not feel any physical pain. In one scene, she was having surgery awake with no anesthetic, talking on the phone without flinching as if pain did not exist. Then the things that would stop her emotionally dissipated in time. She was fearless and no thought interfered nothing could stop her. She was operating in full spirit mode by the end; she was limitless and invincible.

What stops us from ever knowing our fullest spiritual being? Our bodies (physical) make demands, and if our souls (mind/will/emotions) side with the body, then our pure spirits get lost in the abyss. When we were babies, we did not know fear, doubt, or worry, we were ultimately taught by whoever raised us and society at a large not with malicious intentions, but intentions to protect us from what they previously went through. The difference is, you do not have to accept that version of reality. You can create your own.

If you believe you are made in the likeness and image of God, The Creator, a higher power, energy, vibrations, etc., then you also believe you have that same power to create what you want today. Maybe you do not believe in anything at all, but you believe that you control your own life, and you are correct as well. You create your feelings today, and if you don't, then something or someone else does. In a relationship, you want to be in full knowledge and control of your spirit, because if you are not aware, you can be drained or drain someone else physically and emotionally.

You may have that physical connection with someone, which is the most carnal and minimal of the three parts. You may mentally and emotionally be connected to someone, which in the end is stronger than physical. But the spirit is that knowing, subconsciously confident, undoubtable thing deep down that no one can sway. When you know who you are as a spirit first, and you meet someone else who understands their spirit, that foundation is so much stronger than the two alone.

You can become one and align together. Spirit first.

CHAPTER 3

Celibacy is The New Normal

"To keep health is a duty … otherwise we shall not be able to keep our mind strong and clear."

- Buddha, a Christian girl's blasphemer

My longest consecutive period of celibacy was four years. I had been abstaining on and off since losing my virginity. I planned to marry as a virgin, until I was raped and that possibility was taken from me. I thought that I could get back something that was stolen, and claimed it still existed because I did not willingly give it.

The first time that I actually decided to give myself to someone willingly was out of curiosity. I wanted to see what everyone was talking about. I was pretty sure it was not everything it was cracked up to be, but it did not silence my curiosity. I decided that my first time would be with a guy that I trusted enough. I trusted our bond, our friendship, and our genuine connection. After my first time, the first thought that came to mind was, "I could have kept waiting." It almost felt like it was a waste of time. I did not necessarily have this big expectation, but I knew it had to be more than what it was. So throughout the course of my life, I have abstained on and off. I've had a good amount of break in between. Sex tended to happen only in my relationships. When the relationship would end, heart break began and the side effects to that cycle emerged, and I would decide to practice whatever I thought celibacy was at that time the concept I thought it was and what I learned in the church. Same cycle over and over again. You can say my celibacy journey was wishy washy. Ridiculous, I know.

When I was not having sex, I would think maybe I should again, then I did and it was never worth it. I always based my decision off of whether I could see a future with this person. If I was in a relationship, I trusted that we were not going to break up and would eventually get married, so having sex was just part of the "girlfriend" job description. It also never came from the guilty "I'm sinning" mindset, because I never held that type of self-guilt over my head. After I came to a different understanding of my own when I got a little older, my stance changed a little. I understood what now developed into my own definition of celibacy. I knew why I was truly doing it and I became more in tune with myself. I became more vocal about it in my dating process, and of course was met with plenty of criticism.

The criticism was based around the idea that most people stop having sex as a bargaining tool in order to gain a commitment from someone. Some would just laugh or flat out believe that it was a lie. During the now four-year process, I have had to learn how to gain freedom in my personal journey. First, I had to let go of the guilt I imposed on myself, then I had to let go of the guilt and perceptions that came from others. That was my real freedom in celibacy, and it spilled over into an overall freedom in every single area of my life. In dating, celibacy is a choice, but also know that it is a choice for someone else to not care for it. Sex or no sex, people are out here hurting and attempting to love others. With sex comes responsibility. I do not care how you slice it or dice it or if you hit it and quit it. Not matter how you view sex, you have just allowed another person's energy in your space. Celibacy was just a part of my healing process from past pains that I could have kept ignoring. It removed a distraction.

This part of the book could have easily been called abstinence is the new normal for me. Celibacy just has more of a ring to it. Not everybody agrees with the definition of the word, but in my research it doesn't have one operational definition. Celibacy is a word that varies amongst beliefs and cultures. It is used interchangeably with abstinence.

My ultimate definition of celibacy is a form of a detox, similar to my previously mentioned fast. A detox for physical, emotional, and spiritual health. It means denying yourself of your immediate carnal desires to seek something greater, deeper, with a stronger spiritual connection.

Celibacy being the new normal came from the stance of accountability creating a community of people who agree and can encourage one another. Celibacy is a difficult choice without support, especially if you are constantly discouraged by others. Only you know how you feel and why

> **I believe that *abstinence* is a response on the outside to what's going on; *celibacy* is a response from the inside. It should be a period of clarity, confidence, security, and empowerment that you give to yourself first.**

you made the decision. Of course this is just my story and feelings; everyone views sex differently based on their personal experiences. Yes, I wanted to marry as a virgin and it was my goal. No one could have told me otherwise. I did not see me giving myself to just any and everybody. I just wasn't built like that. It just didn't make any sense to me. I have always been this way, outside of how I was raised.

Discrepancies

As I progressed, I started to not be a fan of commonly taught traditions in the church, notably the idea that a deed makes you more holy, and if you do not get "favor" from God it's is because you do not deserve it. The more deeds you do, the more God is pleased. It does not even have to be from the heart, it just has to be good enough, or at least appear to be. This idea was all just word of mouth passed down for generations. It had nothing to do with God and everything to do with people trying to make God have human feelings. You can't humanize God. Tradition speaks for God as if it were a direct order. Then tradition has you sitting around with all of this guilt trying to figure out why you did not get "blessed," believing that the bad things happened to you because of something you must have not done enough.

Although I wanted to be a virgin when I married, that was something more instinctual for me than it being taught to me. Actually, my own mother has always been open to talking about sex in a very clear concise way for me even as a child. It was not something I feared, but it was something I understood on the health side of it. I do at the same time realize that even if you do marry a virgin, you still may not get to this point of self-love, self-actualization, and purpose in singleness. As a virgin, you still may over or under value sex in a different way.

Now let me tie this back into the dating and celibacy world. Some will tell you that you are single because God is making you perfect for your spouse, so you do all of these good deeds and actions hoping that you will get the results. You hold out from sex so that if you do get a spouse you can say, "See I have a spouse now, because I did not have sex before marriage." What about the people who did have sex before marriage? How does that statement even make sense? So now you have others feeling guilty because they are still single. They become resentful if they are holding out on sex, or they become guilt ridden if they are not. I am not a fan of that mentality. According to this way of thinking, you are not celibate to attain spiritual growth, you are actually celibate to attain a spouse. This mind frame still misses the mark.

Some see marriage as a prize that you win by doing enough good deeds. I am not a fan of that mentality, either. Young people should be taught to be single and embrace their time with themselves. It is a gift singleness has value just as much as marriage. Singleness is not a curse, nor should it equate to anything negative. You are not lacking because you are single. That is like someone telling you that you are not enough on your own. You do not become complete when you marry. A spouse is (hopefully) an addition to your life, not a completion factor.

Priorities

What I learned in the end was how to separate spirit, soul, and body, as I mentioned previously. Fasting introduced me to the separation, and celibacy helped solidify them as three distinct elements. In dating, could you stand being around this person as he or she is without the sex? Do you have a deep enough bond that transcends that short period of gratification? When asked to list loyalty, looks, sex, trust, and honesty in order of importance, sex tends to be towards the end of the majority of people's lists, yet we place so much importance on it.

An article I read said we spend .45 percent of our lifetimes having sex. We spend 117 days out of an average 25,000 days in our entire lives having sex. That's assuming you live to the age of 69. Compared to going to work, spending time with love ones, conversing daily with your significant other, sex pales in comparison of time spent in your lifetime, yet we let it be such a forefront in our situations, from seeking sex outside of a monogamous relationship, to letting it be a deciding factor of being with someone or not.

Any choice you make is ultimately yours. It is ever so important to be happy with "self" first. Then hopefully you meet someone who is happy with themselves. If you are already with someone, but you are beginning or on the path of purpose, this goes for you too. Learn yourself. Learn your likes and dislikes. Learn your wants and needs. Find your purpose. Spring full force when you find it! In the end it is not "happy wife, happy life," it is "happy you, happy two."

I encourage celibacy, or what I call a detox period, so it can be prioritized correctly. Only you know what that is for you. It can be a form of discipline to yourself to know that you are not easily distracted a discipline that can create a faithfulness to yourself. If you can be faithful to yourself, you can in turn be faithful to your Creator, and subsequently be faithful to your relationship with someone else. That faithfulness comes in the form of self-control. Self-control helps you master the soul. It starts with you. Sex is put on such a high pedestal, whether for it or against it. For me it has been a great form of clarity. I know the motivation behind my decisions with a person. It creates a very clear line of separation when it comes to who I encounter. I handled situations for what they were, I knew my emotional threshold like a best friend.

CHAPTER 4

Why Men Can't Commit

• • • • • • • • •● ● ●• • • • • • • • •

"I am not giving my 30s to someone who is not ready."

- My Facebook status on May 24, 2016

• • • • • • • • •● ● ●• • • • • • • • •

In three years, I interviewed over 1,000 men and women, formally and informally. I was really curious about the common stereotypes that we hear all the time. Men can't commit, women are emotional, men are taught to sow their seeds before settling down, women are taught to keep her "numbers" low, etc. The common theme that transcended both sexes were four categories: career/purpose, finances, health, and relationships. That was the goal everybody wanted the balance of all four. Three out of four worked, or even two out of four. If the financial, health, and career goals were not met, the relationship always suffered.

I decided to ask six basic questions to see if there was a trend between the genders something a little more foundational. Beyond the initial chemistry, compatible personalities, and laughs, what else do you need to sustain? The answers are not absolute, and of course there are exceptions to every rule. These are just the results from the people I polled. The answers were said by over 70% of each gender.

Interview Questions

Q: Which do you do first in relationships, work, or friendships: Trust or Commit?

A: Men: Commit.

Women: Trust.

So the majority of men said commit? Hmmmmm. So that means without knowing everything about a situation, they are willing to commit to a situation and trust it over time. So men can commit! Men will commit as long as there is not something that gives them that red flag of untrustworthiness. This is not to say that things do not happen along the way, but they are at least willing to be there in the beginning.

As for the majority of women, they said trust. They have to trust someone to commit. The funny thing about that is, the issue could be flipped to say that women are the ones with commitment issues, just not in the common way that the phrase is used. Women can be in a situation without a commitment in hopes that a commitment comes along. She trusts and hopes that it will happen if she is in it long enough.

Commitment is having a common goal to work together and never give up on each other. Commitment is staying long after the mood has left you. Trust is being able to believe and rely on your partner's words and actions that those words and actions are protection from harm or failure. These two things work together in a relationship and are vital to its survival.

Q: What's the number one thing you look for in a mate?

A: Men and Women: Honesty, Trust, and Loyalty.

This seems fairly simple. Keep putting the qualities

you want out there and do not let experience jade you. How do you expect certain qualities from someone that you yourself refuse to display? Do not be the person looking for honesty while being dishonest, looking for someone to trust while being untrustworthy, and looking for loyalty while being disloyal.

Q: What things make you commit to a person?

A: Men and Women: Ambition/Passion, Confidence.

Men: Support, Appreciation, Respect.

Women: Security, Encouragement, Attentiveness.

Your first goal in life should be to find out why you are here on this Earth and where your true passion lies. What is something you can do every day without ever getting tired of it? What lights your inner fire, gets you excited, and brings you more lasting joy than temporary happiness? That thing is everlasting that's your purpose. Once you know what that is, there is no way you cannot walk on this Earth with daily confidence that exudes from within.

Once you have that on lock, I would encourage

> **You know exactly who you are and why you are here, and no one can tell you anything different.**

everyone to communicate with themselves. Better yet, write a letter to yourself. What does support look like to me? What does security look like to me? Write a list under each quality you want in a partner, so that when you do come across someone, you can effectively communicate what those characteristics look like to you individually. Although everyone gave their answers, appreciation looks different to each person and so does respect. Write down what it means to you and communicate what your definition is to the person you are with or getting to know.

Reading *The Five Love Languages* by Dr. Gary Chapman is a good starting point. Even if you do not read the book and you just take the quiz, it helps you understand what your definition of love looks like.

Q: What makes you pull away or shut down?

A: Men and Women: Being secretive, lying, or too emotional.

To me this seems obvious. My thing is, if you cannot be truthful, why can't you just stay to yourself and leave everybody else out of it? All you are doing is creating a trail of heartbreak and tears. You are contributing to the very problem you do not want. Are you too selfish and want what you want right now? What is stopping you from being 100% honest?

In reverse, if you are being honest and you see that someone you are with is falling for you, politely speak on it and pull away. Do not keep dragging on a trail of hope and expectations. The day that you see it is not what you want, end it. The truth does hurt, but the truth is like a sprint it's better than a marathon of lies.

Q: Do you fear marriage?

A: 94% of Men and Women said no. They stated that they mostly feared divorce, not marriage, as well as trusting someone with their whole heart.

So outside of people disagreeing with the social construct of marriage, how it came to be in today's society, and how it is just a piece of paper, people still want a partner and a family unit. My dad always said, "yes marriage is just a piece of paper but only if you want to reduce it to such. Money is also a piece of paper, and I want both."

Q: What do you really want?

A: Men and Women: To be cared about, trusted, committed to, believed in, supported, and appreciated to have feelings equally reciprocated.

We all want love. It's okay to admit it.

Single Reflections

At the end of the 6 questions, I asked those that are single for more of their thoughts, feelings, and experiences about dating. Here are some responses:

"I'm tired of dating someone for two or three years. You meet my family and I meet yours, then it doesn't work out. I want a companion; I want a friend; one that takes time to melt into me."

"The older you get, the harder it is to date. It was easier to date in your teens and 20's. As you get older, the more fear sets in and the more baggage you have. The fear happens after you have been scorned and you question every move the next person makes."

"People don't take seriously the words they are saying out of their mouths when they recite vows. It needs to be agreed that both of us have the resolve to know that divorce is not an option. From day one, it needs to be that if I am spending time with you, it's because I see qualities in you that I want in a spouse."

"I never had a girlfriend in my adult years because I never saw the purpose. I had my first girlfriend at age 18 or 19 and she became the mother of my child. Even then, I was just immature and wasn't ready to handle a serious situation at the time. But after we broke up, I said to myself that I wasn't doing that anymore. The next woman I dated would be my wife. I even had conversations with my friends as to why they got married because I realized that some of them didn't even like the women they were with. They said they just wanted her right now and that she was cute. I never understood the cycle and decided to get out of it."

"I don't fall for perfection; I rather drown in potential. Someone I can help build, mold, and grow with as they push me toward the same."

"I think we are in boyfriend/girlfriend relationships too long sometimes. If you keep a plant in a little plastic container that it came in from Home Depot,

it would eventually die, even with nourishment because the roots have nowhere to go. You can't keep a relationship in the same pot forever or it will eventually die."

"I don't see a point in rushing into marriage. I think a person should be completely content in the state of their lives before introducing someone into their equation. Another person should only add to your life. There shouldn't be any compromising in yourself. Not to say you shouldn't compromise in your relationship, but you should have stuff in line before you get in a relationship. I shouldn't have to kill a part of myself to be with you and vice versa. She should be exactly what I need and I should be exactly what she needs. Like bringing the best out of a person, but you shouldn't be muting parts of yourself for another person. I think our generation is making slower decisions based off what we are seeing, experiencing, and fear. Whether we've seen our parents divorced or our home boy cheating on his wife; those factors are slowing down our process. I don't want to get it wrong and end up with my life changing in a way it shouldn't have. Unforeseen changes are an issue for the ill prepared. The only way I know how to operate is through experience; which is a combination of other things that life has taught me. I just know

that I want to be the happiest version of myself and I want them to be the happiest version of themselves. Our time is very short and we should act accordingly. Getting caught up in anything unhealthy does not help us to act accordingly. You can bring the best out of someone or you can bring the worst out of someone. If it's heading toward the best, then it's a great direction. I don't expect the full package up front but there has to be a foundation to build on."

"I think the answer can be so different for so many people. For some, I think it may be that they think about that person all day; the first thing when they wake up and the last thing when they go to bed. They feel that they have some emotional connection or one can say that it's time to settle down. A person may feel it's in their best interest to marry, be it financially. That person may provide security, support, or various reasons. In any case, I think that it isn't one for all or all for one. Marriages are different based upon what people feel they need in their life at that time. For example, most men need to be settled in their career or financially stable first. She could be a good woman but if he isn't near where he needs to be financially, that will cause him to be more reluctant in moving forward or miss out on a great woman because *of those things that he has to handle. I'm not sure from a woman's perspective but I can say that for me, being financially settled first is important."*

Married Reflections

The one thing that a lot of couples summed up was that everyone makes mistakes. Not mistakes such as repeated cheating when you want a monogamous relationship, or physical/emotional/verbal abuse those things are not mistakes. When you're dating someone, I am sure they are going to make a mistake. When you marry someone, they are going to continue to make mistakes. Someone is going to get frustrated with your mistakes but the key is don't quit in the midst of the mistake. Stick and stay.

"What is love? Love is a commitment without a guarantee. Relationships are 100/0 which means you go into it with no expectations. When you have no expectations, you have no room for disappointments. He is going to give his all unto God because he made that commitment unto God. His wife gets the benefit of everything because his commitment is to God and God alone. The 100 is for God and his wife gets the benefit, even if she doesn't do anything a day in his life. He expects nothing from her. People should go into marriage

and a relationship with love knowing that it is 100/0; all of you and none of them because it's not about them. I asked my grandfather what's the hardest part of marriage and he said the first 100 years. Could you really love someone and commit to someone who gives you nothing? With men, a lot of the decisions they make depends on who their male role model was instead of how they would want their children to be raised. They see the male that raised them or the male that they looked up to and that's how they treat situations instead of thinking how I want my daughter to be treated or how I want my son to be treated. Men need to switch their focus to that."

"Unconditional love is loving the unloving. Marriage is work, every day. It is a continuous discovery, not an end all."

"Being committed to a person is hard. Not necessarily at first, but as time moves on. Through the hurts and offense enters the hard times which every relationship has. There have been many times where I would have packed my bags and left and him too, I'm sure, but our commitment to God and each other allowed us to work things out. Marriage is two imperfect people that refuse to give up on each other."

"We have had some twisters and if felt like the storms wouldn't stop. We have just found a way to protect ourselves from them as you would in any storm. You have to just use intuition, your heart, and prayer. That's how you know. I was engaged to another man and I thought he was the one I was going to be with for the rest of my life. There are always signs in your relationship. Make sure you're not blinded by a love mask. It takes more than love to keep any relationship strong. I was wrong. After two and a half years, I went from a high of new love to a low of no love. When I look back, I never felt for him that of which I feel for my husband. Your spirit will guide you and let you know. It has to be more than just a following of your heart. When your heart, spirit, soul, and body align, then you will know. It will be easy to love. No resistance."

"I knew I wanted to spend the rest of my life with my wife when I met her. I only had the courage to embark on that journey when I truly understood what God considered love. 1 Corinthians 13 taught me that I can display those characteristics towards my wife from day one and that scripture is a great way to describe marriage."

My Reflections

> ➤ **Fear of being hurt creates that thing we view as a commitment issue.**

Learn to take a chance, be fearless. Smart, but fearless.

> ➤ **Not knowing who you are presents a great issue.**

I believe one of the biggest challenges facing men and women in the dating scene is SELF not knowing who you are, where your passion lies, and your everyday purpose.

> ➤ **Be the person you want to be with.**

Do not contribute to the cycle of things you do not want to see in your relationship.

> ➤ **Break away from stereotypes and do not become a stereotype.**

Not all men do this, and all women don't do that. Pay attention to the individual and adjust accordingly.

> ➤ **The only thing that keeps couples together are two people who want to be in it.**

It is really that simple.

CHAPTER 5

Accountability

"Stop giving the same person different opportunities to disappoint you."

- Social media meme

I knew the first time he lied to me. I knew when I confronted him that he would deny my evidence and continue with another lie. I wanted to believe him.

You can either run with your truth and what you think you know, a.k.a. move on, or you can keep confronting it over and over as the same thing keeps happening. You can either become a private investigator going through their phone, checking their email, trying to figure out passwords to their accounts, or you can just ignore everything, believe him, and hope for the best.

I dated a man I could cater to, yet he was emotionally unavailable. Maybe it was my competitive nature that made me think that the more I did, the more he would see my effort that he would one day cater to me as well. That maybe my actions would rub off on him. That through my actions he would see my heart. Maybe if I stuck long enough, he would see my loyalty. Or if I stayed consistent, he would see what love looked like, and in return, maybe he would become emotionally available.

This last go round of dating I attempted something different. I challenged myself more than anything. I could have made this about all of the things he did that were completely wrong, but that would still not hold me accountable for my part in it. Yes, recognize when someone is not treating you the way you deserve to be treated, but at the same time, recognize what you can do differently when you feel this way.

This time I was 100% up front with my intent. I did not want to date just to pass the time. If my dating intent was to get to know someone for marriage and his was just to have fun, I was going to run. I was up front from date one.

> **I want to grow with someone, build with them, learn their greatest passions and their greatest fears. I want to know everything.**

I did not want to waste his time, nor did I want him to waste mine. I want just one person I can talk to every day, not a bunch of pointless conversations with a bunch of temporary people. I wanted someone who wanted to be with me as much as I wanted to be with him. I was ready for something more. I asked all of those uncomfortable questions we tend to avoid so early on:

What is your dating intent?

What is your view on marriage?

What is your view on family?

The things that I deemed important to me, I asked. He seemed to be excited and on the same page. Over time, his tune changed. In the past, this is where I use to get stuck and would completely gloss over the change as if I could not feel the shift. I would operate out of routine to keep the relationship going, even if my gut was telling me something different. Being more experienced and aware, I actually paid attention this time. I learned a lot more about myself. Some would say that in this last situation, I stayed longer than I should have, but I disagree. On the outside, it looked like I dated someone for a year and a half with absolutely no title attached. On the inside, what I saw was a shedding of my old ways and developing a closer bond with *The Knowing.*

I believe that God gave us an internal tracker to guide us. It is something I have learned to trust more and more through experience. I used to ignore it, deny it, avoid it, and flat out detach from it. I did not know that God placed it in us to protect us, warn us, and even encourage and lead us to greater things. It is a knowing observer over your life. I had to stop believing the lies I told myself that I knew did not internally sit right. I call this internal tracking *The Knowing.* It is your spirit giving you a reaction in your soul; you can feel it.

know·ing

/ˈnōiNG/ *Adjective*

1. showing that you have special knowledge

2.   a: shrewdly and keenly alert
     b: indicating possession of exclusive
     inside knowledge or information

To get your attention, *The Knowing* can give you a warning that makes you feel nauseous when you're perfectly healthy. To build your confidence, it can make you feel excited when you are absolutely frightened. It is that voice within that says, "Dang, I knew shouldn't have" or "I should have followed my first instinct" after you've done something you know you shouldn't. And when you do something that went exactly how you pictured, you would say to yourself, "I knew I was right, I could feel it." It is that feeling that no one can take from you. No one can tell you anything different against *The Knowing.*

I was soon tested. My first test was patience. Do I follow my heart and mind like I usually do, or do I attempt to trust *The Knowing?* We started dating, and in month four I came across my first test. I did not hear from this man for a few days. On the one hand, I could have taken that red flag and ended it, on the other hand, I wanted to be considerate just in case something serious happened to him. My old self would have reacted right away, but my new self just waited. When I heard from him, he gave me an explanation that could have been true or false; I may never know either way. It was not about him at this point I was happy that I had matured into this space.

The next test came around two months later when he canceled a date and I became real defensive about it. In my mind, I could not see how expressing how I felt about being canceled on could warrant such a nasty response. Something did not feel right. I did not know what it was I just knew it was not right. This time I did not ignore it, it was just duly noted. Two more months went by with no issue, until I saw something again. It was a message via social media. A message from someone I suspected prior. The kind of message that makes you give the person you are dating a side eye. Now I had visual evidence, but it still was not enough to say if something was happening or not. I asked my brother and he said, "Don't sweat it, but if you see something pop up again then you need to ask about it." So that's what I did. I kept living my life. All the while I started to detach myself from this man emotionally, because although I had no concrete evidence that he was doing anything else, *The Knowing* kept me alert. I paid attention to *The Knowing* this time and was learning to truly trust it.

A few more red flags popped up over the next six

months. A year and a half later, everything came out in the open. Everything I had suspected over the past 10 months was all true. He was dating someone else, even though he always said he was not. The issue I had was that he took the opportunity away from me to make a decision. If he would have said upfront, "yes I am dating other people" then I could have made the decision on what I wanted to do moving forward. He had me thinking I am hopping in this dating ride solo with him driving. Instead, I'm in this ride with other women and acting like I don't know because I want to believe him. If I confronted him, then I was the problem, I was tripping or insecure. He tried to make me think I was the one being immature when in actuality, he was the one selling a world of faux possibilities. Needless to say, I let it all go. I knew better this time around and I knew not to let someone make me question my own sanity. This man probably thinks I was heartbroken and upset, but I tell you, I was beyond elated. I felt a freedom, a joy, a peace. My sanity was back and that heavy feeling was lifted. I knew, like I knew, like I knew all along! I could finally trust *The Knowing!* I'd always had it inside of me, but I was not close enough to it to be familiar with it and use it. This year and a half was not about him, it was about me! I got to see that when I ignored the red flags, I was ignoring *The Knowing*. It was like I had an outer body experience and I could watch my old self meet my new self.

gas·light

/'gasl/

verb

1. manipulate (someone) by psychological means into questioning their own sanity

This is something to watch out for and to recognize what it looks like. If someone makes more excuses than effort, pay attention. If you ask a simple question and they try to make you feel like you said something completely wrong, pay attention. If someone is telling you that you are worthless and not good enough, that is a form of gaslighting. If you do not see the person you are with often and when you ask to spend time with them, they tell you you're clingy, that's gaslighting. If the person you're with disrespects you in any fashion and you confront them, and they flip it back on you, making you feel guilty and apologize, that is gaslighting. Anything that makes you question yourself and what you truly know in your gut can take a psychological toll.

I would have followed my typical pattern: met him, took off like a rocket, and then crashed and burned. This time, I took a chance without the title to see where I usually go wrong. I made myself accountable for my decisions, my choices, and my reactions. I was able to see how not to be argumentative and how to talk to myself about my feelings first, so that I could express them properly and logically. I was slow to anger, slow to react, and slow to jump to conclusions. I learned that the title does matter, but it only matters when you are on the exact same page as your partner with the same goal. I learned that I do not have to have concrete evidence to move on. Most of all, I learned to trust *The Knowing* 100%.

When you ask someone why their relationship ended, most people like to list the things the other person did. Well, what did you do? What was your part in it? Be accountable for your choices, actions, and decisions. You cannot control another person all you can truly control is yourself and your actions. You cannot be mad at anyone but yourself for trying to believe that the person you're with is capable of handling what they were not equipped to hold: your heart. You have to be honest enough with yourself to not ignore red flags, and not try to make the person fit into the box you have in your head. Truth hurts, but long lies do substantial damage to the soul. Stop being delusional, you know better. Stop trying to convince yourself something is there that is not.

When I talk to divorced couples, I always ask if there were any red flags before they got married, and the majority of the time the answer is yes. I have talked to people who said on their wedding day they had nothing but "NO" in their guts but went through with it anyway. If you see the signs and the red flags and choose to ignore them, that fault lies with you. You know what you will and will not be able to deal with. Do yourself a favor and trust *The Knowing* this time around.

You Are a Beautiful Woman

> *"We raise girls to see each other*
> *as competitors—not for jobs or*
> *accomplishments,*
> *which I think can be a good thing—but*
> *for the attention of men."*
> - Chimamanda Ngozi Adiche

To go further into her message, she states that

we condition girls to aspire to marriage but we do not condition our boys to aspire to marriage. This already creates a terrible imbalance at the start. The girls will grow to be women who are obsessed with marriage. The boys will grow up to be men who are not obsessed with marriage. When the relationship begins, it is already unbalanced because marriage matters more to one than the other. This is how women lose themselves in sacrifice.

Below are some notes I wrote to myself over the years. Some are simple reminders, others question why some things are the way they are and how they can be changed. It starts with us and our mind frames. The best thing we can do as women is love one another, support one another, and encourage one another.

- ➢ Life is too short to feel unappreciated. If you are not getting what you want from someone, simply give it to yourself.

- ➢ It is not fair to expect someone to come into your life and fulfill it.

- ➢ You cannot force someone to change or care. Everything another person does is their personal choice.

➤ We will all make mistakes in life. Wisdom comes from accepting it now, learning and growing from it, and making better choices ahead.

➤ Men are not scarce, and as a result, they are not a prized possession to compete for.

➤ Your purpose in life is not to get a winning role in some man's life. You have a greater purpose and greater goals to achieve.

➤ Two is better than one, so focus on yourself until someone comes along and elevates your now.

➤ If you do not like what you are attracting, continue to elevate yourself until what you want is attracted to you.

➤ Do not value becoming a spouse more than valuing knowing yourself and your purpose.

➤ Your relationship with yourself sets the bar of how others treat you. That includes your family, friends, and yes, your relationships.

> ➢ If you want to attract a different type of man, you have to be a different type of woman.

> ➢ Even if you feel like you are becoming a different type of woman, know that that same type of man cannot talk to you anymore, but you are still elevating to be that woman to make room for a new type of man to approach. Continue to evolve.

> ➢ Do it all for yourself, love you first, respect you first, and be confident and proud of yourself.

CHAPTER 6

He Was Never Yours

• • • • • • • ● ● ● **●** ● ● ● ● • • •

"When you are with someone, you don't have possession of them, you partner with them."

\- Something I had to tell myself over and over again

• • • • • • ● ● ● **●** ● ● ● ● • • •

How many times did you sit up crying because someone you were dating called and said it was over? Or you found out that they were cheating on you with someone else? What could lessen the hurt of yet another breakup? Another failed attempt at love? You wouldn't sit up and cry all night if you realized that they were never really yours in the first place. You would not worry about losing love, because you would know that you never had it. You do not own or possess another person. You partner with them. Some make good partners; others make bad partners. Does it hurt? Yes. Do you lose possession? No.

In all-or-nothing relationships, we tend to think in extremes. Everything tends to be black and white. Simple setbacks seem like complete failures. When a relationship ends, you feel like your world has ended and you do not know how to come back from it. It is as if everything has been taken out from underneath you. It is a mental trap. If you do not give yourself the grace to keep going and pushing, you'll fall into that trap every time. But if you think of it differently, remembering that you cannot lose what you never had, then that mentality will create a bounce back effect and it will feel more like a trip rather than an outright fall.

When two adults are in (or not in) a relationship, you cannot control them you cannot tell them what to do. All you can do is control yourself. You cannot control their responses and you are not responsible for anything that they do. You are only responsible for your actions and what you do. What you can control is what you tolerate and put up with. What they do has nothing to do with you and everything to do with who they are. Face it, we all struggle with self-control daily, so why would you try to control the actions of another person? You are resistant to change yourself, yet you make it a priority to change someone else.

> **People were never meant to be owned.**

You can have a possessive nature over a person if you please, but do not be surprised when you come out disappointed on the other side. Your whole focus, and your end goal, should be to be the best you and be great at that every day. Prayerfully, the person you date will match the greatness that you already set for yourself. And guess what? If they don't, you are so focused and in love with yourself that you will see it as a mismatch.

When you are busy working on yourself, you do not have the impulse to criticize other people. You paralyze your future by either not growing while worrying about changing someone else, or not letting go when you are growing.

When you realize what you had was not yours in the first place, it may help you avoid needless drama and heartbreak. Because in the end you can't lose something you never had.

Journey to Healing

• • • • • • • • ● ● **●** ● ● ● • • • • • •

"People will shout their lies with confidence, while suffering in their own truth."

- More inner thoughts

• • • • • • • ● ● **●** ● ● • • • • • •

Life. Everybody has a story. Everybody has something that affects them that shows up in a different form today. You have patterns and habits that were formed from experience early on. You may not even remember what all of those experiences are, but they show up in different areas of your life now.

Like most, I went through my share of pain and

disappointments. I was all about letting go and forgiving easily. I did not hold grudges and was able to move on quickly from things that I did not consider life or death. My mom taught me to never go to bed mad, and if something was wrong, we needed to handle it in that moment. That was not always a good thing, especially when emotions were running high. But I understood her mentality. My dad died abruptly in a car accident when he was 28, and at that time, my mother was 25. Since then, she makes sure that everything and everybody is on good terms because you do not know if that is the last time you will hear from them.

Although I was able to let everything go and forgive, it did not stop me from creating cycles in my own life. So now in dating, if I go into a situation expecting someone is going to be there, then he needs to be there. If he leaves, then I am upset. I feel like he has given up. I cannot go back to exes because even if we decided to get married, I could not trust that they would not give up on us in the marriage. I always believed in pushing through and sticking things out. If I say I am going to do something, then I am going to do it. If I put my heart in it, then I am going to see it through. There are women who say every man they meet is the one. I see where they're coming from because if they have their hearts in it, like I did, then they could really feel like that person is the one. For me, all of my boyfriends could have been "the one," but they broke up with me and once you break up with me, there is no going back because my heart is no longer in it. I cannot conjure those feelings back up again.

That last relationship when I was 27, the one that started me on this path of self-discovery, made me think of that 14-year-old girl with so many questions for her pastor and started journaling. I've spent days pulling out all of my journals over the years and I've realized that my core values and beliefs have not changed. I have always loved love, I have always wanted it for others, and I always have encouraged it it was something I could talk about every day and not get tired of it.

I also noticed in my writings another theme moments that created fear, doubt, and worry in my life. As I sat there, I tried to go through my own life and identify my first memory of pain. I wanted to see if I could recognize any lingering wounds and pinpoint the root of my pain. I decided to visit a pastor that a friend referred me to who was also a psychologist. I was reluctant, but hey, what else did I have to lose at that point? He proceeded to ask me a series of 50 short and simple background questions. In the end, he said my two biggest fears were abandonment and rejection. I was surprised at the accuracy as he went into detail.

Since my father died the same year I was born, when I was 9 months old, I experienced a form of abandonment at a young age, even though there is no way I can remember the experience itself at such a young age. Moving forward, he listed several experiences from my childhood in which I felt either rejected or abandoned and how they affected me as an adult, especially in my relationships.

My mother was a strong woman and I always had great father figures in my life after my father died. Each of them undoubtedly influenced my adult behaviors. The father I first remembered and was raised with, the man I called dad, died when I was 15. The next man, whose last name I have now, became estranged from me after he and my mom divorced. Two fathers dead, and one alive yet distant. It is interesting to think of now, but I am glad that the pastor pointed out this pattern. It allowed me to face my pain and truly heal.

I started to understand why I always wanted

just one person. I wanted a form of stability. I started to understand why every time I got into a relationship, I was in it forever from day one (good, bad, or absolutely terrible) and stayed in it. I just did not want to be left or abandoned by another man. It stemmed from issues that had nothing to do with the men I dated at the time and everything to do with me and my childhood. I was so thankful to come across this pastor because he showed me how to spot my weakness and directly relate it to its root.

Change Starts with You (rewind to 2 years ago)

In order to stop a cycle, you must first start with you. In William McDowell's "Song of Intercession," there is a part in the song that says, "The change I want to see must first start with me." Now, Willy said something there. Yes, he's talking in the big picture about changing the world for God, but what I hear is, if I want to see something different, I must look at the person in the mirror, and that person is me. I noticed my cycle around 12 months ago and have made some slight changes but not anything significant enough from where I am today; I'm still single. Change had to start in my mind, because I had to get my perspective right. I could continue dating while giving the person that I was with the best of me and in the end, still end up where it all started (by myself), or I could do something about it. After doing a self-assessment, I figured out that being by myself was best. There were some things that I had to first correct within myself. I started keeping a self-assessment journal. I literally wrote down what I said and what I should not have said that day. Something as simple as, "Did I say anything positive today?" or "Did I say anything negative today?"

I would write those things down to pay attention to what was coming out of my mouth on a daily basis. Your words have power, so you must watch what you say because you reap what you sow. If you sowed seeds years ago and wonder why you are going through something today, that is because you are harvesting what you previously planted. It does not matter how much good you do on the Earth, or how many affirmations you have been making; what you said two years ago may come to pass. If you said that you were broke then and you are broke now, that is your seed being harvested. It does not mean those thoughts and words cannot be switched expeditiously, it means you really need to make an effort to change those thoughts in your subconscious. I made it a habit to write down my thoughts so that

I could see where I was going wrong and what I could do to improve.

When I looked back at what I wrote down, I learned a lot about myself and what I thought of myself. Things were beginning to change, and this was the start of my freedom experience. I started reading more than usual. I had a hunger for self-improvement and a deeper hunger for the things I had already known but on a deeper level. I started off too deep. I was trying to write down every thought and it became exhausting. There was no way I could keep up with every thought. Then I learned balance.

What steps are you taking on your journey to healing? Can you see where the wounds started?

> **I learned to make the best effort each day, and even if I was only taking baby steps, I was content in that as long as I stayed steady on the path toward improvement.**

It may not be easy to look in the mirror and admit it to yourself. At the same time, it is very necessary to get to the point where you know yourself in and out. It is the beginning of truly loving yourself, flaws and all. By now, you should be able to see some habits that need to be changed and some cycles that need to be broken. The journey to healing can help you put a lot of things into perspective. Try to find the entry point to your hurt.

So now I ask you to do the same reflection for yourself:

> ➢ When was the first time you were hurt or experienced some type of devastation?

> ➢ What was your first traumatizing experience? Do you see how it affects your interactions now?

> ➢ Do you have a fear of loss? Fear of rejection? Fear of abandonment?

> ➢ Can you see the cycle in your life that could have come from that painful experience?

> ➢ Can you identify other past hurts that have affected you deeply?

> ➢ Can you identify where fear stems from in your own life?

➢ Have you recognized some destructive patterns in your life?

➢ Are you ready to change those habits and patterns for the better?

Your self-dissection is your journey to healing. It is a journey to finding out exactly who you are, how you got the way that you are, and how to go about healing any broken parts. If you have been answering these questions truthfully and really searching deeply, you have already found some of your habits and patterns that may not be working out in your best interest. You have started to change your thought process and have to evaluate all of your relationships with family, friends, strangers, and find the common themes.

The journey to healing is not an easy one. It all starts with the first step, whatever step you feel like is appropriate for you and your situation. Whether it is speaking to a professional or in a nonbiased setting, it is important to get it out. The deeper you go into the journey of healing, the further you stretch into a bright, peaceful, resilient future.

If you want to change your life, you have to start with you.

CHAPTER **8**

13 Actions

"I didn't fall in love, I rose in it."

\- Toni Morrison

What is love? Is it an action or a feeling? I know I mentioned before that feelings don't last long. If you were mad about something last year, I'm sure that today you couldn't conjure up the feeling that you felt back then. I can think of something that made me mad four years ago, but today there is no feeling attached to it. Yes, it was intense four years ago but it was a fleeting emotion. It came and it went. The memory was there, but I could not bring the feeling back, especially if I have moved past it. Then it made me think, if feelings don't last long, how could love be a feeling? If love is a feeling, how can you keep that feeling going with a person you are with? Actions. Love in this chapter is a series of actions. It is a series of things compiled. Some believe you cannot love someone without showing those actions first to God. These actions are wonderfully mentioned in 1 Corinthians 13:4-8. Honestly, I think the best practice with each part of this passage is to practice each part on yourself. Practice these sections to see if you can even give them to yourself before you attempt to give them to someone else.

The actual word "love" may not fall in the front of each phrase mentioned in scripture, but it would help if, when reading it, you place the word "love" in front of each phrase that is used to describe what love is for a deeper understanding of this writing.

> "*4 Love is patient, love is kind. It does not envy, it does not boast, it is not proud. 5 It does not dishonor others, it is not self-seeking, it is not easily angered, it keeps no record of wrongs. 6 Love does not delight in evil but rejoices with the truth. 7 It always protects, always trusts, always hopes, always perseveres. 8 Love never fails.*"

Love is Patient

Ask yourself, can I be patient?

Here's an example: you have a 3-year-old child, niece, or nephew. You're at home, and that little terror is ripping and running through your house. Of course you may feel how you feel, but the child is family and you love him or her. Now let's take this same scenario, but instead it is your friend's 3-year-old, or better yet a stranger's child ripping and running through your house! Now that patience you just had with your family does not exist for someone who is not family. You get it? That's patience.

When you're in a relationship, you tend to give yourself more grace or patience than you give the person you are just getting to know. It is like a teacher who starts you at zero and all of your scores equal up to your average, versus a teacher who starts you off with an A and marks you down for everything you do wrong. You can never get back to that A, and she does not offer you extra credit.

See, if you give yourself the grace or patience of the first teacher, you can always work your way up to a better score. But if you treat people you do not know (or are getting to know) like the second teacher, they can never get that same grace you give yourself.

Let's take driving as another example. How much patience do you exercise before you blow your horn at the car in front of you that hadn't noticed that the light changed or that cut you off? What about exemplifying patience when the person you're dating doesn't answer their phone? Where is patience then? I think we can safely say that if we are to ever be perfect in love, we have to start by practicing patience in all things.

Patience is just the first one. Love is patient, pause. I can literally just stay on this first description and see where I have failed at loving others. This one action alone stops so many people from truly loving another.

Am I patient with my parents? Am I patient with my significant other? Am I patient with my kids? Am I patient with my friends? Am I patient with my coworkers? Am I patient with complete strangers? Am I patient in a line at the drive thru? Patience is love.

Love is Kind

When you think about being kind, do you think

about that warm and fuzzy feeling you get from being nice to someone, like walking a sweet old lady across the street? Or paying for the groceries of someone behind you in line without them knowing? Kindness has different aspects to it that you may have to work on. Are you kind to your close friends and loved ones but rude to strangers? Or in reverse, are you rude to your friends and loved ones but kind to strangers? If I'm kind here, but I am only a little bit kind there, then maybe if I learn to be kind in all areas, it would help my love journey as a whole. Try being kind to someone that is always pushing your buttons. It is easy to be kind to someone who loves you back, but what about practicing your love walk with those who seem unlovable? I believe that is a great way to strengthen your love muscles, by working on those that add resistance. Try being kind to someone who is not so kind and let his or her actions teach you how to love through that action.

Love Does Not Envy

How does it make you feel when you see your significant other having casual (not disrespectful) conversation with someone else? Does a jealous or envious feeling arise in you. Do you not want them not talking to, hanging out with, or being in the same room with certain situations because that bothers you? Do you have a possessive nature and you want to be with that person day in and day out because you cannot handle the thoughts in your head when they are not with you?

Or on the flipside, do you see "relationship goals" and want what someone else appears to have? Even though you do not know the ins and outs of another's relationship, you still want it based on what they show you. Although no two relationships are alike, you steadily compare your relationship to others that you think have more than you. Instead of being thankful and grateful in the situation you are in, you hurt yourself and your relationship by envying others.

Proverbs 14:30 states that "envy rots the bones." With envy, love dies inside of you and it rots and kills your relationship.

Love is Not Boastful or Proud

How many times have you dated or been in a relationship with a self-absorbed person? They went on and on about how great their job was, or how they graduated top of their class 20 years ago, or that they just bought this really expensive car.

But they don't even know the basics about you, not even your favorite color. Love is not boastful or proud. Boasting is a trait that you find in men and women. While there is nothing wrong with letting people know what you have accomplished in life, when asked, it's not a great idea to always throw it in people's faces just because you can. I have found that being boastful and proud can go into more of a negative ego direction than a positive one.

If you think you may exude this, can you think back on the times when you had nothing to boast about? Get into your humble state. Remember your lowest points and how you broke through them. If you've never had a lowest point, go volunteer at your local homeless shelter. If you are at your lowest point now, appreciate every breath you take and know that, as cliché as it sounds, the light is at the end of the tunnel. Everyone has heard the statement "do not forget where you come from," or "humble yourself before you get humbled." Both mean that meekness keeps you grounded and forever thankful. That is another area of love, one area that is often forgotten.

Love Does Not Dishonor Others

For the sake of this aspect of relationships, we

will consider dishonor as failure to respect. First, are you respecting yourself? Are you being the best you? Are you honoring your word and carrying yourself to your highest standard? If not, you cannot even begin to expect the person you are dating to give you what you are not giving yourself. Can you take yourself out on a date without getting tired of being with you? Can someone look at you and automatically know that they cannot treat you a certain way based off how you carry yourself?

When it comes to relationships, how do you act around others? Do you respect the person you are with, or do you berate and belittle them because of what they aren't or haven't done for you? How much respect do you show them when you are out with your friends or family members? The same respect that you are showing them may be the same respect that you are showing the person you are with. That person is not your property that person is your equal.

In friendship, how are you speaking about the people you call friends? Are you talking about their character, intent, and heart to others in a negative fashion? Or are you talking to your friend directly? How you handle situations shows whether you are honoring or dishonoring the people you call family or friends the people you claim to love? How can you tear down and ruin the reputations of those you are close to? If you are dishonoring others, recognize it and do better. If you are being dishonored by others, go where you are celebrated, not tolerated. True love does not dishonor or disrespect others. It's always looking to honor others.

Love is Not Self-Seeking

Are you selfish? In a relationship do you think about your needs before your partner's? Are you more of a receiver than a giver? That is self-seeking. It is thoughtless, inconsiderate, egocentric, and self-serving. It may be so normal to you that you do not even realize that you are making your partner feel unloved, unwanted, not respected, or even insignificant. Self-seeking is a big character flaw when you are in a relationship. It can explain why so many people get hurt. That is not a good trait to carry into a relationship because if it is all about self, then that other person will get hurt. People have to realize that they are not the only person in their relationships. They are dealing with another person's heart, and a union like that has no room for self-seeking characteristics.

Love Does Not Easily Anger

You may be a person who just snaps. You may get angry and shut down. Sometimes you may even explode. Someone may write you off as crazy while you call yourself "passionate." You may feel like, "You see my loyalty, and that I have your back regardless, right?" I have never felt that there was someone on this Earth who had my back all of the time, but I could go down a list of those I was behind 100%.

It's easy to say, "If you don't want your partner to be angry, then don't do things that would anger them." For example, if you are in a relationship, don't talk to your exes if this angers your partner or yourself. That seems to be one topic that gets a lot of people in trouble these days. If you are with someone, then that means they exemplify the characteristics you want in a person now, so why are you talking to your exes? It will only cause confusion and heartache in the long run. You may not even want to cheat, but why play with fire when you can eventually get burned. Exes are just an example; the same applies for complete strangers. What seems good in a moment could burn for a lifetime.

This also ties directly into to patience. It is not

always about you and not always something you should take personally. If you perceive something as wrong, sit back, and let it happen. What is done in the dark does come to light, so you should not worry about it. Let it play out. It is not worth your energy to get angry about things you cannot change. Do not discuss things in the heat of the moment. Let time cool your anger.

Love Keeps No Record of Wrongs

This part right here is tricky to me. We can say that we forgive and forget, but do we really forget? It is hard not to keep a record of wrongs when your mind does not forget easily. Honestly, it is hard, but it will just take some work and time. Take it one day at a time. Sometimes you live in your own guilt and are not quick to forgive yourself. You may have an, "If I had not done this" or "If I could take this back" mentality. You have not forgiven yourself and you are keeping a tally of your own wrongs. How on earth can you forgive the next man when you are still putting yourself on a fault scale?

Do you keep bringing up the past every time you get upset? Are you always focused on what happened instead of forgiving and moving forward? Do you use absolute phrases like you "always" do this when it is not always, or you "never" do that when it has happened before? This record of wrongs goes hand in hand with forgiveness. We are not forgiving our partners, we are just steadily marking them down. This is a big topic that ends relationships because people can't seem to forgive one another. You have to forgive. Not only for that person, but mainly for yourself and the greater purpose of the union.

Love Protects, Trusts, Hopes, and Perseveres

These four words are amazing together: protect, trust, hope, and persevere. Having all of these together will ensure that love stays pure. Real love encompasses these traits and many more, but if we take our time with love, we will see how to be perfected in love. Do you really trust someone else with your wellbeing? Are you hopeful of your future with this person? Do you trust them with your future? Do they even see a future with you behind the broken promises and empty words? Can you persevere beyond any obstacles you two may face? And what about protection? Everyone has a sense of protection built within him or her, but the protection of a partner for you is just unexplainable.

Love Never Fails

Love never fails. Love is always there for you, always wanting you to be the best you can be. Love is there to constantly tell you who you are and who you are not. Love will never give up on you, disappoint you, degrade you, hurt you, disrespect you, lie to you, or think the worst of you. Love does the absolute opposite. It builds you up. It smiles at you. You enlighten love. It loves you. It cares for you. It is always seeking after you. Love is the Creator. If you have failed in love, then you have never let it love you properly. For God is love!

So What is Love?

Love is not this uncontrollable feeling. Lust can be uncontrollable. Attraction can be uncontrollable. That tingling feeling in the beginning can be uncontrollable. Love is all of the actions mentioned combined. None of these actions focus on personal desires. Can you see what areas are your strengths or what areas are your weaknesses? Are you impatient and easily angered, yet you keep no records of wrong and you protect your relationship like a pit bull? Well that still is not a totality of love. It is a series of all 13 actions...

Patience
Kindness
Not Envious
Not Boastful/Proud
Honors
Selfless
Not Easily Angered
Keeps No Records of Wrong
Protects
Trusts
Hopes
Preservers

...working together. When you choose to display all 13 actions, love will never fail. I can see now which areas are the weakest for me and why I cannot give those areas in a relationship. For me, I know my points, which include patience, keeping records of wrongs, and trust to an extent. If you do not give me a reason not to trust you, then I will trust you. But it is a gut feeling, *The Knowing* spirit that you are trustworthy.

Too many people ignore their intuitions, their true knowing spirit selves. Outside of the obvious red flags that they can see, they ignore the red flags that the Spirit gives them. They may know that they don't feel good about a certain situation or person, yet they move forward anyway. That in itself is a lack of love for themselves, through the lack of patience. As you can see, the actions of love all intertwine and need to be recognized and practiced. You have to know yourself in order to fix those areas you lack in love. First recognize all the attributes it takes to love, then practice love.

God is Love.

I AM... Patient

(a prose poem)

My confession of impatience led me to its foundation. Growing up my mother never told me no, to anything. I thought I could have whatever I wanted when I wanted it, technically I can, but with patience and not with force. I always had good grades, so I stopped studying and just did enough to get by. I catch on quickly, so I ignored teachers, employers, and eventually authority in general. There was always a shortcut in life, in my opinion; I had to find the easiest route. As an adult it spilled over into my everyday life. When driving, I would ride down the right turning lane just to cut everybody off and get by. Well, the side effect to my impatience led to interrupting people in the middle of their sentences or trying to finish their sentences before they did—thinking I know it all and tuning people out trying to convince people of my way of thinking so I could have my way. When this reality hit me, I started to speak another I am. Instead of sitting in my own way I declared that day ... I AM Patience.

OUTRO

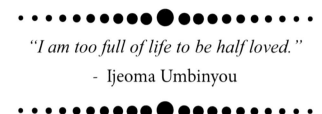

"I am too full of life to be half loved."

\- Ijeoma Umbinyou

Everything stems from that conversation that I had in my pastor's office at the age of 14 when I asked him, "What is a girlfriend?" Inside I knew that I was not girlfriend material because I did not know what that looked like back then. I had the mentality of committing forever, and I still have that today. I did not go into a relationship seeing an end. I did not understand how you could say you love someone and not see it through. With that mentality, I took breakups very hard internally.

There is nothing wrong with wanting that love. In the end, whether people admit it or not, they want it too. The only thing that has changed in my adult years is how I get in it, how I look at myself, and how I set the tone for the person I'm dating. Knowing what I can

> **My wants are still the same as they were at 14: to have a partner who wants to be in it as much as I do—someone who will never give up on us.**

control, and not being wounded by the things I can't.

How are you in your dating life? Yes, you can get to know a person, but it's time to get to know a person with a clear intent. Over time when that friendship develops, you have to choose if you can seriously see yourself teaming up with this person. Does this person make you a better person? Do they inspire, motivate, and add value to your life? Do they help you think? Do they expand your horizons for your betterment? Do they have your best interest at heart? You have to find out the foundational parts about a person and what matters to you the most. Would you want them to be the parent of your child? Is raising a family important? Is how they handle finances important? These are all factors that need to be taken into account when getting to know someone with clear intent.

Chapter Reflections

Chapter 1: I Want the Title

Do titles matter in the end? In my opinion, yes. Titles matter when it comes to your education, your career, your home, and your car, so why would it not matter in a relationship? As much as people like to water it down, they are doing that to protect their own hearts in order to not be vulnerable. Others may be avoiding the responsibility that comes with the title in a relationship. Whatever you want, you will gladly accept the title that comes with it. So if you really want to be with a person, the title will not bother you.

Chapter 2: Spiritmates

You are a powerful spirit being. The bible says you are born with the same spirit that raised Christ from the dead (Romans 8:11). If you believe in Christ or not, that statement in itself should give you a picture of the powerful spirit that you are and that resides inside of you. Your spirit has no limits, no boundaries, and it can take you wherever your heart truly desires. Tap into it.

Chapter 3: Celibacy Is the New Normal

Figure out how you view sex. Depending on your view, prioritize and value it correctly for yourself. Be honest with yourself on what you can and cannot handle. Most of all, I encourage that detox period so you can truly discover who you are spiritually and have a clear separation between spirit, soul, and body.

Chapter 4: Why Can't Men Commit?

Men can commit, so can women. Everyone wants honesty, respect, appreciation, and dependability. If you want a commitment, communicate that. If that person is not willing, it is your responsibility to move on.

Chapter 5: Accountability

Be accountable for staying longer than you should have stayed or for ignoring alarming red flags. Write a list of negotiables and non-negotiables for yourself what you can and cannot deal with. Once you have a list, you will able to spot those flags sooner. It is your responsibility to act on it.

Chapter 6: He Was Never Really Yours

Yes, just like a business, a relationship is a partnership; a team. You would not get into business with someone that you could see failing from the beginning. In a relationship, you should go in it with a similar outlook. Outside of the connection and emotions, could you truly see yourself partnering up with this person? Most of all, remember that you do not possess or own them. This is your equal and potential life partner.

Chapter 7: The Journey to Healing

Find out what first caused you pain, doubt, or disbelief. Get to the root of it, heal from it, and remove the limits that it has caused. Find that common denominator. Recognize how it has affected your friendships and relationships.

Chapter 8: 13 Actions

Love is a series of actions. All of these actions work together. Figure out which actions you need to strengthen. Find out what actions you need to give yourself first. And when you partner with someone, figure out what actions they need to feel loved. Yes love is work, and with all these actions working together, love cannot fail.

I LOVE love! I want everybody to believe in it again! I want everybody to have it! I want everyone to be happy in it!

In the end, your own actions can prevent needless heartbreak. It begins with truly knowing yourself spirit, soul, and body. Start by discovering your passion and figuring out your purpose. Dig deeper to heal past hurts and do the exciting journey of SELF-DISCOVERY. When you know yourself and know what you want, KNOW there is nothing wrong with what you want! Rise in love with yourself so that someone knows how to fall in love with you.

BONUS CHAPTER

Limitless

· · · · · · ● ● ● ● ⬤ ● ● ● ● ● · · · ·

"Being realistic is the most commonly traveled road to mediocrity."

- Will Smith, forever The Fresh Prince

· · · · · · ● ● ● ⬤ ● ● ● ● ● · · · ·

You know what I miss? The old me. Not me from a few years ago, I mean birth me. The fearless me. The childlike, innocent me. I miss the limitless being I was before the world and society taught me fear. The society that taught me to fear based on the experiences of others and used fear as a mechanism to protect those who came after them. We tell kids, "You can do anything you set your mind to" and in the same breath say, "You can do anything, but not everything."

I want to get back to that stage where mental boundaries did not exist. As a child, if you wanted to jump off the bed, you jumped; you did not think about the possibility of getting hurt.

> **Innately, whatever you wanted as a child, you demanded it as if it were already yours.**

As a child, you had to be taught doubts, consequences, and overall negative alternatives to thinking. Wisdom does come to play in this, so I am not speaking of things that have true consequences. I understand that if you murder someone, jail or worse can be a consequence. I am referring to the things that were taught to you that dimmed the light that you are. Those things that threw shade in front of your beacon.

I am speaking of those things that stop you from being where you truly want to be. They start in your thoughts and words. I want to unlearn the negative while keeping the wisdom from the positive things I learned in life through time and experience. I want that for you too to get to that place where you do not think or speak limits over your life. Your thoughts and words are the keys you need to free yourself from your own mental prison. It's time to retrain your brain.

Did you ever hear someone say, "I'm just being realistic" or "This is just reality?" Well here's the good news: what someone else says does not have to be your reality. You can change your current reality.

"REALITY is everything that has existed, exists, or WILL exist!" -Wikipedia

Well, look at that! That means that things that have not come to pass yet are a part of reality. Now let's add faith

"FAITH is the confidence that what we hope for will actually happen; it gives us assurance about things we cannot see."   Hebrews 11:1 NLT

So with FAITH we can create a new REALITY of things that we want to come to pass. You may or may not have heard of affirmations, but this is why they are important. Affirmations are statements or declarations that you stand on. You say these words or phrases to build yourself up, encourage yourself, and lift yourself up. Even when you do not feel like it, these words repeated over and over again eventually trickle down to your feelings. It is very important for you to speak to yourself daily until your own words make you a believer in your mind and heart. You may be "broke" today, but if you continue to say it, you will believe it, and create more of it. You are not waiting on something to be done that something is waiting on you. It's already done you just can't see how. You have to align your thoughts to the finished product and let God do the rest.

Who:	You
What:	Your words and thoughts
When:	Now
Where:	In your heart and mind
How:	Not your worry
	Not your concern
	The "How" is a Greater Power, it is greater than you.
Why:	Because this is how you change your reality

On the relationship side, watch what you say. Do you say things like, "I will always be single," "Nobody wants me," "I can't find anybody," or do you say things like, "I can find whatever I want," "What's good for me will find me?" Listen to how you talk to yourself in regards to being with someone. It is also important for you to be in control of your feelings. You create your feelings. If you are not in control of your feelings, then that means that something or someone else is in control of them. Find out what that is, take power away from that thing, and regain control. It takes practice but it is the key to your peace.

If only you knew the power behind your thoughts and words. This is not a new concept, but I am going to repeat it again. If only you knew the power behind your THOUGHTS and words. What we focus on, speak about, feel, and act upon, work together to create our strengths and our limitations. Our inability and ability to know ourselves is what causes us to be more dominant in one area in our lives, and less dominant in others. Only you decide your limits, so pay attention to your thoughts and words. Do not tirelessly pick through each one, but notice your pattern. Start with baby steps to see how you can change your way of thinking.

It is not too late to change. Even if you have been practicing positive thinking and positive speaking, you may feel like you are not seeing the results. For some years, your words and thoughts have unknowingly planted negative seeds in your life and you're trying to figure out why, now that you're positive, you are still seeing the same results. Well those negative seeds are still harvesting from past thoughts, so all you need is enough patience to wait for the positive seeds you are currently sowing to come to fruition. Others around you may see the negative harvest as disappointment, and that disappointment is something what people call "reality."

Reality is safe, reality is comforting, reality does not take chances, reality is mediocre. Reality remembers the things we should be forgetting in the now: the mistakes and the failures, and reality forgets what we should be remembering: the successes and the victories. Pay attention to what plays in your mind over and over again like a highlight reel.

I just want to list a few common quotes, sayings, phrases, and verses that show you that life can be changed. When you change the way you look at things, the things you look at will change. That change starts in your mind first. Whatever is in your mind, your mouth follows.

➢ "Death and life are in the power of the tongue." - Proverbs 18:21

➢ "If you believe it, you can achieve it." Remixed by a lot of people

> ➤ "The only thing that is keeping you from getting what you want is the story you keep telling yourself." Tony Robbins

> ➤ "Think like a queen. A queen is not afraid to fail. Failing is another steppingstone to greatness." Oprah Winfrey

> ➤ "Speak those things that are not as though they were." Romans 4:17

> ➤ "If you believe, you will receive whatever you ask for in prayer." Matthew 21:22

> ➤ "There is a truth deep down inside of you that has been waiting for you to discover it, and that truth is this: you deserve all good things life has to offer." Rhonda Byrne

> ➤ "Whatever is true, whatever is noble, whatever is right, whatever is pure, whatever is lovely, whatever is admirable if it is anything excellent or praise worthy think about such things." Philippians 4:8

> ➤ "You become what you think about most. But you also attract what you think about most." John Assaraf

This list can go on and on. The point is that what you think about, you bring about. Write a list of goals, long-term and short-term. Write things out that you want to see come to pass. Create a vision board. Write a list of "I Am's." Whatever works for you, do it today. My morning routine includes saying "Thank you" repeatedly when I wake up. I say "Thank you" when I am looking in the mirror, brushing my teeth, and washing my face. Then I drink a whole bottle of water and follow it up with a protein drink. After that, I go into my affirmations. Find the routine that works for you. Find that thing that gets you going as soon as your eyes open for the day. Find that thing that changes your energy and puts you in a peaceful joy.

In order for me to visualize or see something different, it starts with my words. Those words help me see it in my mind, which is followed by believing it in my heart. Belief may not happen overnight. It took you years to think the way you think now; it will take time to change that pattern.

Your new reality now includes those things that WILL exist. So start adding those things that are not yet here to your list. Whatever it is, speak it now. Remember you are limitless, you have no boundaries, you are amazing, and you can have whatever your heart desires!

Affirmations

Below are a few affirmations that you can begin with. Use the lines below to add additional affirmations that you can repeat to yourself daily.

I AM AMAZING

I AM UNSTOPPABLE

I AM THE BEST_____

I AM _____

I AM _____

I AM _____

I AM _____

I AM _____

I AM _____

I AM _____

I AM _____

10-Date Theory

I have heard dating described as collecting data. I thought that was a cute way to look at it! I started to think, when I am dating, am I really collecting "data" or just winging it in the moment? Then I found something interesting, the 10-Date Theory. The 10-Date Theory states that when two people start dating, only 50% will reach the second date and only 10% of those pairs of people will make it to the 10th date. That speaks volumes! That means you can avoid moving further with a person than you need to by following this 10-Date Theory.

A first date is important for clarifying intentions. Go to random locations, outside of the home, where you have time and space to exchange information and collect the data that you are really seeking before making permanent decisions with someone. A date can include a coffee shop, a restaurant, or a nice picnic in the park under the tree, but whatever you decide, just get creative.

> **There are a lot of things you can do outside of the house in order to gather the necessary data to see if this person has the potential to move further with you.**

Some people say that going on that many dates does not happen anymore and that it doesn't exist, but it can exist if you make it exist. One day while watching the movie *Hitch*, the person I was watching it with asked if things like that really happened these days all the dates he planned, how he paid attention to her likes and wants, and how he courted her and won her over. I responded by saying, "it happens if you make the effort to make it happen." Plan a date and make it happen! It's just that simple. It does not take much effort at all, nor does it always have to cost money. We always want convenience in today's society. Everything is instant. Instant meals in the microwave, online shopping, instant movies from home you don't ever have to leave the comfort of your own home. Your relationship can't be the same way. Take the time to collect important information regarding a future with a person instead of bypassing the collecting data phase and jumping straight to the feelings phase. That's where the confusion sets in. Take a step back, get out of the house more, and stop hiding behind technology. Maybe you will meet somebody the 1995 way.

Date Ideas:

- ➢ Go take a nature walk

- ➢ Go to a park and take pictures of what you find beautiful

- ➢ Find a free festival

- ➢ Miniature golfing

- ➢ Go to an art museum

- ➢ Walk around a city and have a makeshift photo-shoot with your cell phone

- ➢ Pick strawberries, apples, or whatever you can pick where you live

- ➢ Go to a beach or creek

- ➢ Go roller skating

- ➤ Go bowling

- ➤ Share your music playlist and memories

- ➤ Find a nice coffee shop

- ➤ Find an open mic night

- ➤ Go bike riding

- ➤ Indoor Skydiving

- ➤ Carving Pumpkins

- ➤ Find an Escape Room in your city

- ➤ Feed the homeless together

Write down any of your own ideas below:

_____

_____

_____

_____

_____

HAPPY DATING!

INSPIRATIONS

Hey hey hey! These are books and articles that helped me during my healing and self-discovery journey. They have also inspired me to write this book about my view on love and dating. Hope you enjoy!

How to be Led by the Spirit of God by Kenneth Hagin

Instinct by T.D. Jakes

The Alchemist by Paulo Coehlo

The Five Love Languages by Gary Chapman

The Four Agreements: A Practical Guide to Personal Freedom by Don Miguel Ruiz

The Holy Bible

The Laws of Thinking by Bernard Jordan

The Miracle of Right Thought by Orison Swett Marden

The Power of Now by Eckhart Tolle

The Secret by Rhonda Byrne

Understanding the Purpose and Power of Woman by Dr. Myles Munroe

When a Woman Finds Her Voice by Jo Ann Fore

You Are a Badass by Jen Sincero

REFERENCES

"Flapper." Definition of in U.S. History. N.p., n.d. Web. 29 Sept. 2014.

Fellizar, Kristine. "How Much Time You Spend Having Sex in Your Lifetime." How Much Time You Spend Having Sex in Your Lifetime. N.p., n.d. Web. 25 Oct. 2015.

"Knowing." Merriam-Webster. Merriam-Webster, n.d. Web. 25 Oct. 2016.

Jain, S. A. "Reality." Wikipedia. Wikimedia Foundation, 03 Oct. 2016. Web. 25 Oct. 2016.

The Holy Bible. Nashville: T. Nelson, 1989. Print.

McDowell, William. Song of Intercession. 2011. CD.

Hitch. Dir. Andy Tennant. Columbia, 2005. Film.